TIES THAT BIND

Ties that Bind

FIBER ART BY ED ROSSBACH AND
KATHERINE WESTPHAL FROM THE
DAPHNE FARAGO COLLECTION

ESSAYS BY PAUL J. SMITH AND JAN JANEIRO
CHECKLIST BY SUSAN HAY

MUSEUM OF ART, RHODE ISLAND SCHOOL OF DESIGN
PROVIDENCE, RHODE ISLAND • 1997

TIES THAT BIND
*Fiber Art by Ed Rossbach and Katherine Westphal
from the Daphne Farago Collection*

The RISD Museum, Providence
October 17, 1997 – January 11, 1998

The American Craft Museum, New York
June 25 – September 6, 1998

ISBN: 0–911517–64–2
Library of Congress Catalogue Card Number: 97–74303

COVER: Katherine Westphal, American, b. 1919, *New Treasures from Tutankhamun*, 1978 [cat. no. 55, detail]

BACK COVER: Ed Rossbach, American, b. 1914, *John Travolta*, 1978 [cat. no. 20] (photo courtesy of Mobilia Gallery, Cambridge, Massachusetts)

FRONTISPIECE: Ed Rossbach and Katherine Westphal in Luxor, Egypt, 1970 (photo courtesy of the artists)

Contents

Foreword 7

Introduction 9

The Fiber Art of Ed Rossbach and Katherine Westphal 11
JAN JANEIRO

Katherine Westphal and Ed Rossbach:
Reflections on Life and Work 21
PAUL J. SMITH

Biographical Information 41
PAUL J. SMITH

Checklist of the Exhibition 45
SUSAN HAY

Foreword

In 1980, Ed Rossbach and Katherine Westphal were invited with eleven other artists to Rhode Island School of Design to weave on the School's antique Jacquard loom. As part of a National Endowment for the Humanities program organized by the RISD Textile Department's Alice Marcoux, Rossbach and Westphal, neither of whom had any experience on this type of power loom, each designed a "point paper" (a diagram showing how the loom should be programmed) and wove lengths of fabric that were then exhibited in the RISD Museum (February – March 1982), as was the work of the others in the program. This was an exciting first chance for our students and public to get a look at the actual work of these two artists.

Thanks to the generosity of Daphne Farago, the Museum is again able to present the work of Ed Rossbach and Katherine Westphal, this time in a two-person exhibition of far greater dimension. The pieces on view, all from Daphne Farago's collection, show Rossbach and Westphal's range and imagination – from their efforts in the Sixties to break with established conventions and test new possibilities, right up to the present day, as they continue to create unique solutions to the challenges of making fiber art. Ed, a weaver, is interested in structure, and Katherine, a painter, in surface design. These concerns have spanned their careers as their work has come to a joyous maturity that celebrates their lives and travels together in totally different but related ways. Shared themes in this exhibition include the artists' reverence for the past, their pushing of boundaries, and their reaction to the many different cultures they have encountered through study and travel.

Ed and Katherine are important figures in the contemporary fiber arts movement not only because of the influence of their work, but also because they are teachers as well. Based in Berkeley, California, they have trained a whole generation – from fiber artist Lia Cook to basket maker John McQueen – to follow their individual creative muses. It is particularly appropriate that this exhibition should take place at the RISD Museum, which itself is dedicated to both the exhibition of art and the training of artists. We are thrilled to present the work of Ed Rossbach and Katherine Westphal in the exhibition *Ties that Bind*.

The Museum is grateful to Ed and Katherine for their interest in RISD, their support of this exhibition, and the many insights they have given us about their lives and work. We also thank our two authors, Jan Janeiro and Paul J. Smith, for their fine contributions to the catalogue and their advice on myriad details of the exhibition planning process. The Bancroft Library of the University of California at

Berkeley has allowed us to quote many passages from their oral history of Ed Rossbach. Ann Rowe, Curator, Western Hemisphere Textiles, Textile Museum, Washington, D.C., provided much helpful advice. Holly Hotchner, Director, and Ursula Ilse-Neumann, Curator, at the American Craft Museum, New York, were also of great assistance.

Within the RISD Museum, we wish to thank Richard Benefield, Assistant Director; Linda Catano, Paper Conservator; Tara Emsley, Assistant Registrar; Susan B. Glasheen, Associate Curator, James Montford, Coordinator of Community Programs, and David Henry, Head, Museum Education; Margaret Leveque, Object Conservator; Pamela Parmal, Associate Curator of Costume and Textiles; Pia Restina, RISD work-study student; Judith A. Singsen, Publications Coordinator; Monica Smith, Communications; Sarah C. Stevens, graduate student assistant, University of Rhode Island; and Stephen Wing and James Swan, the current and former Managers of Installation. Thomas S. Michie and Jayne E. Stokes, Curator and Associate Curator of Decorative Arts, took charge of the initial organization and planning of the exhibition, wrote the first version of the checklist, and contributed their insights throughout the project. Susan Hay, Curator of Costume and Textiles, also played an important role in planning and was curator for the exhibition's final stages. Del Bogart, former Museum Photographer, admirably captured the spirit of Rossbach and Westphal's work. Photographer Dwight Primiano stepped in to take a number of essential images at the last minute. Gilbert Design Associates is responsible for the stunning look of the catalogue.

Most of all, we are grateful to Daphne Farago for proposing the exhibition and freely sharing her superb collection with all of us, and to Libby and JoAnne Cooper of Mobilia Gallery, Cambridge (Massachusetts), who represent the artists, for their interest and advice throughout. Without them, we would never have had a chance to see the works of Ed Rossbach and Katherine Westphal side by side in our galleries, nor have been able to mount such a tribute to two great pioneers in the fiber arts.

DOREEN BOLGER
Director
Museum of Art
Rhode Island School of Design

Introduction

WHEN I THINK OF Ed Rossbach and Katherine Westphal, three qualities come to mind: imagination, talent, and integrity. Ed Rossbach and Katherine Westphal have dedicated their lives to fiber art. Their work – always unpredictable and surprising – heightens our awareness of materials that we almost never notice, awakening us to the wonderful visual and tactile qualities of fiber, its variety and richness of structure, texture, color, and pliability. Using the ordinary stuff of everyday life (including castoffs), these artists make art objects that reflect our daily existence in a stimulating and meaningful way, and they do this with humor and honesty.

Their imagination is inseparable from their talent. The virtuoso abilities of Ed Rossbach and Katherine Westphal make their vision and materials come alive in tangible objects that reveal a technical brilliance, but their art goes beyond technique to a profound expression of respect for fiber and to a personal integrity. Their special vision suffuses their work and makes it enduring. It is clear, uncompromising, and complete. They are asking us to think and to realize that *things* – ordinary materials and everyday objects – may be beautiful and meaningful and may even transform our lives.

Ed Rossbach and Katherine Westphal are pioneers and leaders in the field of fiber art. As artists, teachers, collectors, curators, and friends, Ed and Katherine have enriched the lives of many, helped to build the foundation for contemporary fiber art in America, and extended its sway internationally. It is a privilege and pleasure for me to be the caretaker of works by Ed Rossbach and Katherine Westphal and to share them with others. I hope that the pieces on exhibition here will come to mean as much to the show's viewers as they mean to me.

I would like to express my gratitude to the entire staff of the RISD Museum for their help with the organization of this exhibition. Doreen Bolger, Director; Susan Hay, Curator of Costume and Textiles; and Thomas S. Michie, Curator of Decorative Arts, deserve my additional praise for their enthusiasm and dedication to this project. Special thanks go to Libby and JoAnne Cooper of Mobilia Gallery, Cambridge (Massachusetts), without whom my collection and this exhibition would never have come together.

DAPHNE FARAGO

Ed Rossbach and Katherine Westphal at home with their
dogs Molly and Sam, 1992 (photo collage by Katherine
Westphal, courtesy of the artists)

The Fiber Art of Ed Rossbach and Katherine Westphal

JAN JANEIRO

CHARLES EDMUND (ED) ROSSBACH and Katherine Westphal have created artworks for more than fifty years. Their careers as artists, professors, writers, and lecturers have spanned the entire history of what is now called the contemporary fiber arts movement. They have left their indelible imprint on the attitudes and conceptual context that nurtured and gave the movement its protean form. Many of their works have become visual icons that memory conjures [cat. nos. 11, 58] when one thinks of the various and diverse directions taken in the new textiles, and their art continues to be crucial to the understanding of this ancient but ever-changing medium.

These two artists, husband and wife, have expressed themselves in almost every conceivable fiber technique, material, and style with the exception of site-specific installations, monumental works, and collaborations. The exclusion of these three areas from their *oeuvre* is, itself, indicative of their attitudes and their creative processes. They are single individuals who each create a total and unique work directly reflective of their own interests, ideas, obsessions, and lives. The process of creating is more important than the finished work; it is the engaged activity that is essential. As Westphal has stated, "For me, the most important thing is the creativity, the invention, the imagination; not perfecting the thing and making it right. And very definitely, I'm interested in the next one, not the last one."[1]

Rossbach has commented: "I was never, in school or anywhere else, encouraged to work expressively....I never felt that the field was wide open, and that I could go in any direction I wanted to."[2] Over the course of their careers as artists and teachers, Rossbach and Westphal have given exactly that encouragement to others, and this is perhaps their greatest accomplishment. Their work has opened doors to the myriad possibilities of the textile field, which, together with other craft disciplines, began actively reinventing itself during the late Fifties and early Sixties. Generations of their students have recognized and articulated the gift given to them by these two teacher-artists. They "gave permission": permission to explore not only the possibilities of a given technique or material, but more importantly, to explore the ideas and messages of one's own expressive vocabulary in an atmosphere of acceptance.

Textile craft is embedded deeply within the earliest human needs relative to survival and the beginnings of communal social life. For thousands of years there was little technological change in the processes and tools used in textile production worldwide. Textiles preserved a preeminent position as functional necessities, preferred trade objects, indicators of wealth and prestige, and articles of ritual symbolism. The Industrial Revolution in Europe and America drastically altered the age-old production methods of textiles and changed their cultural roles. The invention of the spinning jenny and the Jacquard loom, followed rapidly by the total mechanization of spinning and loom weaving, eliminated the individual from active involvement in cloth manufacture. Once it could be produced quickly and sold cheaply, fabric ceased to be a relatively scarce and valuable commodity and so no longer a medium of iconic expression in Western society.

Ironically, the Industrial Revolution's very success in cheap mass production of commodities gave rise to the Arts and Craft Movement, an attempt to rescue handcraft media from the obscurity into which they had fallen. In England, individuals such as Augustus Pugin and William Morris criticized the lifeless, poorly conceived goods rolling off conveyor belts and campaigned for an infusion of creativity into the design process. Stressing the importance of designers who had mastered the techniques and materials of their domains, the Arts and Crafts Movement gave renewed significance to the handmade object. These ideas were adopted by Germany's Bauhaus school and cooperative, whose insistence on the marriage of the arts, the crafts, and industry dominated early twentieth-century design philosophy. The ideas of the Bauhaus had a profound effect on the major industrial nations, narrowing the definition of textiles while planting the seeds that would lead to an artistic and conceptual revolt during the Fifties. As Rossbach was later to comment:

> [We were] content to work within a remarkably narrow range of weaving possibilities, untroubled by any awareness of what was possible and wonderful in weaving, and untroubled too by the solemn restraints that somehow had been imposed upon us. Small wonder that in a few years a vigorous reaction occurred.[3]

Paul Klee taught his students at the Bauhaus that "textiles are a serving thing." The textile craftsperson was encouraged to create prototypes that could then be reproduced by machinery, prototypes that filled contemporary utilitarian needs. Textiles as a class of objects were deemed synonymous with woven cloth, and cloth was considered only in functional terms. Several generations of textile craftspeople were educated in the "correct" design of cloth for the modern interior – simple in structure and made of efficient new materials that rendered it soundproof, colorfast, long-wearing, and generally unobtrusive. These attitudes shaped Ed Rossbach's formal education in textiles.

Charles Edmund Rossbach was born in 1914 in the Chicago area, where he and his three sisters were raised. The family eventually settled permanently in Seattle, Washington, during the Depression years. Rossbach attended the University of Washington, Seattle, where he received a BA in Painting and Design (1940), and then continued his education at Columbia University, New York, where he earned an MA in Art Education (1941). He returned to Washington State and began his career in education by teaching a seventh-grade class in the small rural town of Puyallup. The attack on Pearl Harbor interrupted this first year's teaching assignment. Rossbach enlisted in the Army Signal Corps and spent the duration of the war stationed in Seattle and the Aleutian Islands.

It was during his one-year tour of duty on the island of Adak that Rossbach made his first rather unsuccessful foray into basketmaking:

> I set about gathering individual grasses and stalks which seemed promising although I had little idea what constituted quality in basketry materials....I achieved no baskets, only a box of selected grasses and a brittle start of interweaving.[4]

More importantly, this experience gave him an insight into the symbiotic relationship of the maker of baskets to his world: "...I continue to value the Aleutian experience, with the insight it gave me into the nature of basketmaking as something related to a place and a way of life."[5]

Ed Rossbach on Adak, Aleutian Islands, Alaska, where he was stationed during World War II, 1944 (photo courtesy of the artists)

Returning to civilian life, Rossbach decided to reenter graduate school. In 1940 he had attended the Golden Gate Exposition on Treasure Island. There he had seen the decorative arts exhibit organized by San Francisco weaver and designer Dorothy Liebes and had decided that he would like to weave upholstery. With no previous weaving experience, he applied to and was accepted at Cranbrook Academy of Art in Bloomfield Hills, Michigan, making use of the GI Bill to further his education.

Rossbach's training at the University of Washington (with Johannes Molzahn, a former Bauhaus teacher, and Amédée Ozenfant, proponent of Purist painting) and at Cranbrook (with the Finnish-born weaver Marianne Strengell) was based on a modernist aesthetic that "emphasized the formal properties of art rather than the pictorial or expressive." In the weaving department at Cranbrook Academy, these theories had become codified into a narrow range of acceptable variations

– only particular weave structures in particular color combinations, and always to create cloth that ultimately became something else: upholstery, casements, clothing.

> At the time I went to Cranbrook – everything has changed since then – the approach to textiles was extremely narrow, with strict limitations on what the students were allowed to weave. By the time I left, I was already rankling under this approach, although I had no idea what I thought textile education should, or could, be. The approach at Cranbrook seemed a dead end…We wove some beautiful lengths within these restrictions – they all said 'contemporary weaving' loud and clear, and they were technically competent and in good taste. Mild good taste.[6]

After two years of study at Cranbrook, Rossbach received his MFA (1947). He returned to Seattle and began teaching textile design at the University of Washington. There he met his future wife, Katherine Westphal, who had a position teaching design and illustration; and Jack Lenor Larsen, a graduate student who had been assigned to be his teaching assistant.

During the summer of 1949, Rossbach taught a course at the University of California, Berkeley (UCB). He was given a permanent teaching position in the fall of 1950 with the Decorative Art Department and continued to teach at the University until his retirement as Professor Emeritus in 1979. The Decorative Art Department faculty at UCB exerted an important influence on Rossbach's work and thinking. Prior to his arrival, the department had been headed by Lila O'Neale (1886–1948), a textile historian and scholar who had done extensive anthropological studies of Central and South American pre-Columbian and later ethnic textiles. Under her guidance the department had developed an immense collection of historic textiles, which was available as a teaching/study resource. Because of her collaboration with several renowned anthropologists, among them Alfred Louis Kroeber, the enormous holdings of the Robert H. Lowie Museum, the University's anthropology museum (now renamed the Phoebe Apperson Hearst Museum), were also accessible for study and classroom use. This was an entirely new world to Rossbach, whose Cranbrook experience was entirely focused on contemporary handweaving.

Ed Rossbach and Katherine Westphal in Greece, visiting the stalagmites of Dikilitash, 1964 (photo courtesy of the artists)

Rossbach recounts long hours spent poring over diagrams of ancient textiles (many drawn by Lila O'Neale) in an attempt to catch up with his new students, who had been nurtured and trained by O'Neale and anthropologist Anna Gayton (1899–1977), for whom industry and even art were of little concern.

I was expected to teach a multitude of techniques, so I learned from books. I admired drawings and diagrams of interlacing threads. I was absolutely fascinated by watching the movement of an individual thread, sometimes floating on the surface and then dipping below. I made my own diagrams and fantasized huge knot structures that were houses with people living in them. I converted some of these drawings into super-sized actual constructions by using rolled newspapers for the elements. I wanted the students to understand structure. Like algebraic equations, their weaving should be based on structural clarity.[7]

The professor who seems to have most influenced Rossbach's own developing style of teaching was Maija Grotell, with whom he had studied ceramics at Cranbrook. She had shared with him her collection of textiles from Finland: "Her response to textiles was so emotional, and so sensitive – it put textiles into another realm of meaning and expression."[8] The wonder and humanity of textiles is what Rossbach so eloquently and significantly communicated to generations of his students. "A special quality of a handwoven textile...is its ability to evoke an awareness that someone, someplace, wove it."

Rossbach also tells a story about Grotell that clearly shows her influence on his teaching presentation and his own creative work.

...She used to do demonstrations on the wheel...[One of the] last times she did a demonstration, somebody said, "It looks hard," and she knew she had failed, because even if the work is hard, you don't make it look hard [because then] it's exhausting to look at.

Forty years after that Cranbrook experience, Rossbach spoke about his own work:

...More and more I don't want my work to be refined and craftsmanly....I like the idea of just doing it in the most direct and simple way, and don't bother with refining it, carrying it into this highest state. I don't want it to be hard, I want it to be joyous.

Rossbach is perhaps best known for his writings and work with basketry. After his Aleutian experience, he made no other attempts to construct a fiber container until his interest was engaged by a student coming to him from an anthropology class. The student referred to a classification system that distinguished between "hard" and "soft" textiles, "hard" referring to basketry forms [cat. nos. 4, 6, 17–18, 21–27, 29–46] and "soft" to woven constructions [cat. nos. 1–3, 5, 7–16, 19]. That chance comment initiated for Rossbach an ongoing engagement with the basket form and a scholarly, historical, and interpretative dialogue that continues to the present day. Although Rossbach's work has incorporated almost every known textile technique and format through the years, the basket somehow seems to most clearly capture the concerns that are the hallmarks of his work: an emphasis on structure, a creative process open to an exploration of possibilities, a conceptual questioning of established expectations, a connection to historical precedents translated into the current vernacular, and an assumption that any material can potentially become the stuff of art.

Katherine Westphal was born in Los Angeles in 1919. She attended Los Angeles City College with the original intent of becoming a commercial artist, but found she was not interested in learning prescribed techniques and so-called "hard discipline." Transferring to the University of California at Berkeley, she completed a BA and then an MA in painting in 1943. Her first teaching job was at the University of Wyoming, where she taught for one year. Returning to the San Francisco Bay area, she worked briefly as an occupational therapist at Permanente Hospital during World War II. In 1946 she was hired by the University of Washington, Seattle, to teach design, and it was there that she met and married fellow faculty member Ed Rossbach.

Katherine Westphal's personal involvement with textiles began in 1950, when Ed Rossbach became a faculty member of the University of California, Berkeley. She began a study of printed textiles with Mary Dumas, a faculty member in the Decorative Art Department. This was followed by eight years of designing fabrics for the apparel industry. In 1966 she accepted a position to teach industrial design at the University of California, Davis. She had assumed that she would only be teaching for a semester, but she stayed for thirteen years, retiring in 1979 as Professor Emeritus.

Westphal began her "serious" textile work when she decided to take the remnants from the many design samples she had created, cut them up, and reassemble them. This fragmenting, layering, and collage process became the characteristic style informing the rich surfaces with which she loves to work. Her art, like that of her husband, has taken many diverse forms over the years – quilts, clothing, jewelry, books, baskets, gourds, drawings, embroideries – constantly changing, evolving, moving on, spiraling back.

> I work spontaneously, emotionally. I just put things together until it seems right to me. It is not an intellectual process in any way. I may start out with something, and it may change its direction very much as I'm working, and I just follow the impulse. I try not to modify. I just let what happens happen; sometimes the pieces work and sometimes they don't. I don't criticize them and try to make them better....

The garment form is one that Westphal has continually revisited over time. Influenced initially by the simple geometric forms of ethnic garments being worn by many in the Bay area during the Sixties, she began making clothing for herself. The flat, untailored forms of the Central American *huipil* [cat. nos. 66–67] or the Japanese kimono [cat. no. 57] were planar surfaces that allowed Katherine to play freely with multiple processes and layered embellishments. This was during the period of the growth of a phenomenon later termed "wearable art." Katherine became one of its prominent spokespersons, but she found that "I could never quite convince people to wear my wearable art. I feel it should be worn because it is a moving thing and it should move and be on people; but people put them on the wall, and they didn't even move the position, they kept them very static on the wall." After this recognition, the garments became suggestive forms: large silhouettes, the shapes of garments sometimes at rest, sometimes in illusory action [cat. nos. 54, 58]. Since they no longer needed to meet the requirements of actual clothing, these works could be giant-sized, backless, formless, of paper instead of cloth. Each "garment" became a canvas that might be drawn upon, stitched, printed with an eclectic arrangement of transfer images, or collaged with a variety of additive elements, following Westphal's dictum of "more is more."

For many years one of the main distinctions between the work of Ed Rossbach and Katherine Westphal was that Rossbach's was structural, while Westphal's dealt with surface design – Rossbach created woven and hand-manipulated structures, Westphal dealt with embellishment techniques. As Westphal herself wrote in 1976:

> When sharing studio space, work does not have to be similar. In the intervening years our outpourings have become more dissimilar. Ed's work is structural, often minimal. The image is most often so abstract as to be thought of as nonobjective. Color is either monochromatic or extremely brilliant. My work is on the surface. It is flowing, overabundant, layer upon layer. The imagery is people and animals and flowers in impossible situations. Color is lavish and rarely has value contrasts. It floats in and out.[9]

This is still true for the vast majority of the artists' output before the 1980s; but since that time, Rossbach has become more involved in the surfaces of his baskets, adding "skins" of transparent papers that have been painted or carry photocopied images and may be stapled, layered, and stitched [cat. nos. 26–27, 39–46]; Westphal has created a series of baskets crocheted with designs that are not additive, but are created by and through the constructive process [cat. nos. 59–61, 63–65, 71, 73–75, 78–84].

Beyond the similarities of recent productions, these two artists have long shared attitudes that have shaped their lives and work in a very profound manner. They are both celebrators of human creativity. They have shared a wonder and a fascination with problems that engage their imaginations and interests. They have disregarded the marketplace and its hype and pressure to pursue their own journeys of discovery. They have recognized the importance of historical roots and connections, but have never mindlessly recreated past forms. Katherine has said, "...We share integrity and dedication to create. We always strive to communicate a message with our personal symbolism. We work constantly."

The artwork in the exhibition *Ties that Bind: Fiber Art by Ed Rossbach and Katherine Westphal from the Daphne Farago Collection* illustrates a history and a relationship. It includes objects selected from nearly four decades of the artists' ongoing activity. Each work incorporates the artist's vision and records the decision-making process that gave that vision its physical form.

Ed Rossbach's pieces from the Sixties and early Seventies (cat. nos. 1, 5, 11, 13–14) illustrate his early preoccupation with time-intensive techniques worked two-dimensionally like minimal drawings. Juxtaposed with these chromatically subdued structural statements are brightly colored creations with recognizable imagery and a wry humor (cat. nos. 3, 9, 15). They are still concerned with structure and use historical textiles as sources, but their high-contrast colors and stylized iconography align them with folk and Pop art. The tremendous variety of visual forms and technical experimentation in Rossbach's works of the Sixties and Seventies gave way in the Eighties

Katherine Westphal posing with Javanese mask while
visiting Bali, Indonesia, 1979 (photo courtesy of the artists)

Ed Rossbach confronting the buffalo outside a Los Angeles
antique shop, 1988 (photo courtesy of the artists)

to a focus on basketry. Usually the shapes are classically simple, but the surfaces are activated by mass-media imagery, bright colors, and eclectic collage materials. They are visually and constructionally improvisational.

Katherine Westphal's earliest piece in the exhibition, *Peruvian Monkeys* (1967; cat. no. 47), sets the visual and technical vocabulary that came to characterize her nonbasketry work, complete with collage, layering, juxtaposed designs playing off one another, and elaborately embellished surfaces. The two quilts, *New Treasures from Tutankhamun* and *Hawaiian Kitsch* (1978; cat. nos. 55–56), also display photocopied images as transfer prints, another characteristic technique that she began experimenting with in the Seventies. This latter process allowed her full freedom to manipulate images from her own photographic endeavors with images appropriated from popular mass-media sources.

Westphal continued using heat-transfer prints on the garment forms of the Eighties (cat. nos. 57–58, 66–67), making that technique another additive element in her complex visual layering. These garment shapes create a sense of tension by being essentially flat fields that allude strongly to dimensional forms; they are alive with "objectness." This object quality is given full life in the series of gourds and baskets of the Eighties and Nineties. Using a single technique – crochet – and a single material – synthetic raffia – Westphal manages to achieve in her most recent baskets (especially cat. nos. 78, 81–82) the same type of visual complexity that she previously created using multiple techniques and materials.

Again, these two artists' works have been moving into both a convergence and a reversal. Rossbach's ongoing preoccupation with a clearly stated construction has currently taken the form of a structure or skeleton concealed or texturally revealed by a tight skin that is printed, painted, and embellished. Surface and form are now receiving equal attention. Westphal's sense of physical layering becomes illusory, embedded in the structure, as one color movement cuts across another and background interacts with foreground. Even with an overlap and convergence of issues and processes of working, the creations of these two artists still remain essentially and distinctly their own; unmistakably and uniquely identifiable.

For the viewers, it is as though these objects have been conjured forth out of air and given magical life. Much of the work seems ephemeral and fragile, made of paper and tied together with apparent carelessness. One may ponder the imagery and the relationship of surface to form, amused by the quirky and irreverent juxtaposition of the abstract and precisely real; but one is surely touched by the sheer joyous abundance of these objects, which seems very far from the high-minded seriousness and narcissism of the majority of contemporary works. These two artists have succeeded in making art "look easy" as it flows into delightful existence.

NOTES

1. Unless otherwise noted, all quoted material is taken from interviews conducted by the author and used as the basis for writing the following articles: "A Way of Working: Katherine Westphal and the Creative Process," *Fiberarts*, vol. 7, no. 6 (November/December 1980), pp. 35–37; "Piece Work: The World of Katherine Westphal," *American Craft*, vol. 48, no. 4 (August/September 1988), pp. 32–39; "Ed Rossbach: Influential Presence," *American Craft*, vol. 50, no. 2 (April/May 1990), pp. 48–51; "Ed Rossbach: Prizing the Journey," *American Craft*, vol. 50, no. 3 (June/July 1990), pp. 40–45.

2. Quotation from Ann Pollard Rowe and Rebecca A. T. Stevens, eds., *Ed Rossbach: 40 Years of Exploration and Innovation in Fiber Art*. Asheville and Washington, D.C.: 1990, p. 16.

3. *Ibid.*, quotation on p. 19.

4. *Ibid.*, quotation on p. 17.

5. Ed Rossbach, *Baskets as Textile Art*. New York: 1973, p. 8.

6. Rowe and Stevens, *op.cit.*, quotation on p. 122.

7. Virginia West, "Ed Rossbach: Embracing the Fabric of Art," *Fiberarts*, vol. 9, no. 1 (January/February 1982), p. 31.

8. Rowe and Stevens, *op. cit.*, p. 122.

9. Katherine Westphal, "Katherine Westphal Says," *Craft Horizons*, vol. 36 (June 1976), p. 26.

Katherine Westphal and Ed Rossbach: Reflections on Life and Work

PAUL J. SMITH

From taped conversations with Paul J. Smith, April 9–11, 1997

KATHERINE WESTPHAL

Formative Years

THERE WAS ALWAYS an art program when I went to school, and I rapidly excelled in art – not in athletics. I hated the time when one was supposed to be out in the school yard playing baseball. I spent all my time drawing....

My mother was interested in cooking and fixing dinner and being a typical housewife of the early Twenties...I was sort of in the way, but she had an ironing board in the kitchen. I would sit under the ironing board and color and cut and paste and make my little creations. She was very supportive, but I think a little amazed that I didn't take to music. We had a cousin who played the piano and sang, and this was my mother's idea. I resented every minute I had to be near the piano, particularly when I had to dust it....

I did not draw in coloring books. I drew on plain pieces of paper when I was a child. I think I may have driven my mother nuts, because I always wanted to know why. I had to know the reason why. There were all these questions. I still question. I questioned authority; I wanted to go my own way.

Junior and Senior High School

BY THE TIME I got to junior high school, I think I was dedicated to art. This was the one thing I wanted to do most – except for roller skating....

I took art every semester that I was at Virgil Junior High School. My teacher Grace Nottage took me to the Los Angeles County Museum and to the section of Chinese ceramics. I've often gone back hunting for the ceramics I saw then. There were all these cases of red and green and patterned vases, but I've never been able to find them again – it was a very vivid memory of all these ceramics, all in rows....

Two nights a week when I was going to high school, I would take drawing at Los Angeles City College. My mother didn't appreciate my bringing those life drawings home, but I guess that's the way mothers were in the Thirties. By the time I got to Los Angeles City College, I

21

was very skilled and doing all these little tricks, learning to draw the "right" way. I think it was my exposure there to art history and to people who had studied with Hans Hofmann that made it dawn on me that there was more beyond doing everything "right" – that you could break the rules.

Los Angeles City College

I THINK PROBABLY the most important person in encouraging me in art was Alan Workman, one of my teachers at Los Angeles City College. He taught the art history courses, and he taught some painting courses, and he had gone to University of California, Berkeley [UCB], where he studied with Hans Hofmann. He opened my eyes to what was going on in the contemporary art world in Cubism and, also, to all this art out there in the world, particularly the art of the Classical world.

University of California, Berkeley

I WANTED TO BE FREE – free from parental restraints. I wanted to move out into the great, big, wonderful world. I don't think I had a specific goal. I thought, "Well, I have to somehow earn a living," and the only possible thought was for me to teach; so I came to Cal [UCB], I took art classes, and I took education courses. I worked mostly with Worth Ryder, who was a painter and who also taught art history. I got to know him very well, and he encouraged me very much. Worth was a fantastically articulate man who made art history classes live. The thing he said that I remember most is, "If you are going to tell a story, you have to make it a good story, whether it is true or not." Of course, this is what he did, and this has been invaluable to me in teaching....

I took classes in what I think was called the "Decorative Art Department" from Winfield Scott Wellington ["Duke"]. He taught a wonderful course called "The Nature of Materials." He had a vast collection of everything: ceramics, silver, jewelry, textiles. He would talk once with slides, and then he would bring you into his large classroom, where he had all these objects – and you could touch them. You could touch a Chinese vase and feel a textile. He talked about the architectural quality of how the material influenced the form. He arranged exhibits in the Berkeley campus power house of material from the Lowie Museum [the Robert H. Lowie Museum of Anthropology, UCB]; wonderful, complicated exhibits, beautifully displayed. I can remember basket shows, Northwest Coast shows, Chinese ceramics shows, Egyptian shows. Wonderful stuff! This was always a highlight of the year, to see what kind of show Duke was preparing....

In my graduate year, I took weaving from Lea Miller. They moved me up to some big antique loom they had, and I didn't like the way it was operating, so I took the thing apart. Lea just looked at me – she was horrified. Lila O'Neale [1886–1948; then chairman of the Decorative Art Department] said, "If she took it apart, she can probably put it back together again." Great confidence!

With Lea Miller you wove samples in all these different techniques – six inches by six inches – on little, tiny looms, and you mounted them on paper. Then I moved on to weaving a rug, which was not stiff enough for a rug, but I thought it was a rug. It was not weaving as art, it was weaving as occupational therapy, or homecrafts, or whatever. At least I learned how to thread the loom, which I hated to do, and to keep it in balance; how to warp, how to untangle yarns: all the important and awful things that you get involved in. Today I can't stand to have anything to do with weaving.

I GOT MY MASTERS DEGREE from University of California, Berkeley, and I got a scholarship. It was called the Phelan Traveling Scholarship for Practicing Artists. Then I got part of an Ann Brenner Prize, and I decided to go to Mexico for a few months. I went with two friends to Mexico City to see all the murals, and we had a letter of introduction from the University with a gold seal on it. Brazen as we were, we called to make appointments to see these muralists, and they saw us! We went to Siqueiros's studio, and I was impressed with his very thick glasses: he had cataracts or glaucoma. His were very violent paintings compared to the very controlled ones of the rotund Diego Rivera. On my jacket I had an enameled pin that I had made, and Diego Rivera was very fascinated with this little pin. I wouldn't give it to him because it was my prized possession, the best enameled thing I'd ever done.

Travel to Mexico on Scholarship

MARY DUMAS WAS TEACHING in the Decorative Art Department at Berkeley. She was teaching a course in printed textiles and said, "Come on down, sit in the classes, and I'll teach you how to do printed textiles." I loved it, and I learned how to do all this from Mary. Then I gathered a group of textile designs on cloth, and I went through the New York directory and listed the names of people I thought were converters and wrote letters. It turned out that Frederick Karoly wanted to see my designs. I didn't know he was an agent, so I sent him the designs, and he immediately was on the phone, saying, "Are those your designs? You didn't cut those off a piece of cloth, did you?" I said, "No." I hadn't known that printed textile designs were done on boards, not cloth. Karoly showed them to a few clients, and they were absolutely fascinated, because they could see how the designs would look when the fabric was draped. Both Ed and I designed for Karoly. It was pretty hectic, but fun. We did a new textile design every day. We each did our own individual ones.

Designing Textiles for Industry

I stopped designing textiles shortly after we got back from Europe, probably around 1957 or 1958. After that time, Karoly decided that he wanted to retire. He sent back all these unsold textiles, and there were lots of them, because Ed and I had been producing, between the two of us, one textile design every day for years. Later on, I saw them, and I suddenly had the idea to cut them all up and put them together. This was how I started doing the patchwork quilts.

Teaching at University of California, Davis

I WAS INTERVIEWED for the teaching position as a result of a the show of quilts at the American Craft Council's Museum West [the American Craft Museum in New York, like its former San Francisco branch, Museum West, functions under the aegis of the American Craft Council]. The powers that be in Davis had picked up from Museum West the fact that I had worked for industry. They were phasing out their design department, but had eight students who still needed a class in printed textiles. They twisted my arm, and I said I would do one class each quarter. At the end of the first year they decided to phase out the department, and they fired me. The students got so enraged that they went to the dean *en masse* and complained. The chancellor said he wanted design in the College of Agriculture; it was important. Suddenly design took off. I continued on and was there another year. By 1968, when I got tenure, we had gone from eight students to a hundred and fifty. By the time I left in 1979, when I decided I wanted to be a full-time artist, we had three hundred majors in design....

It was very free. We tried to get the students to develop their own sense of where they were going. They needed to know how to get informed: they weren't handed little checklists on how to do everything. Everybody taught very creatively, and the students responded to it....

Anything I asked the student to do, I had to be willing to do myself. To avoid this hang-up of "What shall we do?," I would set up a plan in my mind of step one, step two, step three, but this was not rigid, it was a sort of a crutch to get them going. I would try out everything myself. The longer I taught, the less structured my methods became. When I taught, I did not do class criticisms. The students worked, I had a phonograph going, and many times the washing machine would be going at the same time, and we would be fighting mosquitoes – Davis has rice fields around it, and the mosquitoes are unbelievable at certain times of the year. The students were free to work. If they wanted to go sit on the lawn, they could. Then I would bring the work out, one student's at a time, and lay it on the ground, and the student and I would talk about it. I tried not to be critical or say, "That is bad." I only commented on the good things, the things that were individual to the person....

Very often something a student did gave me an idea. I had a student once who sewed all these tie-dyes into long tubes and stuffed them; so I started manipulating tie-dyes into three-dimensional forms. It didn't go very far with me because I was more interested in the flat, but I definitely picked this thing up from a student.

Having Fun

PLAY IS GREAT; it's wonderful. I think that was one of the magical things about the time I was teaching at Davis – everybody liked to play. Spontaneously, things would happen. One person would take up on what another person had done, and pretty soon it had escalated into a parade across the campus, or carrying a palm branch to the dean. Somehow I think we all take ourselves too seriously. We only get a chance to live once, so we might as well have fun doing it....

I somehow think the things we are going to remember are the things that are funny. We're not going to remember the other things. It's all part of popular culture. I'm sure, for example, that Andy Warhol's soup cans will go on forever – longer probably than Campbell's Soup. One of Ed's former students sent us the catalogue from the Andy Warhol show, and I look at it and think, "These things are wonderful. Here he is going back to classical drawings and putting gold leaf on them. How wonderful!"

I THINK COLOR IS FASCINATING, and I love boxes of colored pencils or crayons, or paint or dyes – the bigger the range of color, the better. I'm not as interested in the value contrast as in the chroma contrast....

Color

I am attracted to paintings by Bonnard and Vuillard and Matisse and all these very busy colorists. I love the Gauguin paintings of pink fields...all the variations in the color of pink. When I think about color and use it, if I'm painting a surface red, it isn't red, it is a million reds, with little variations – there is some yellow in it, some white, some dark – it is never one color [cat. nos. 53–54, 64]. There are all these variations and the maximum impact of one complementary color against another. It is, I think, a color contrast rather than a dark-and-light contrast.

IMAGE TRANSFER   All the time I was teaching, I would learn new techniques that I could then show to my students. When you do silkscreening, you laboriously paint tusche [a greasy ink] on a stretched-fabric screen and then put block-out varnish on it. [The tusche resists the varnish; when the varnish dries, the tusche is dissolved with a solvent that does not affect the varnish, creating a stencil that prints the image when inked.] Then came photo emulsions, and the business of doing a kodalith, and putting the image on the screen. Davis had all these photocopy machines. I found out that I could print with the photocopy machine on an acetate sheet and then use this on the screen; I didn't have to go through the kodalith process. That got me interested in the copy machine. The first things I did were not transfers, they were silkscreens. When the color copier came out, there was one available in the science department that the medical school used to make prints for the young doctors. I found out how to use it. I got a grant to work on this, and I went over and used that machine all the time. I printed on heat transfer paper – the same stuff used on T-shirts – then I printed on cloth.

Learning New Techniques

PHOTOGRAPHY   I suddenly discovered photography. I had a little camera and photographed constantly in the museums, because there they allowed you to photograph as long as you didn't use a flash. They were lousy photos, but they were enough, with my sketches and journals, to help me remember things....

I began with a photograph that Ed took of me in Basel. The roof of the opera house there has glass brick pyramids on it, and I ran

Katherine Westphal on the roof of the Basel Opera House,
Switzerland, 1976 (photo courtesy of the artists). Westphal used
this photo in her quilt *Hawiian Kitsch*, 1978 [cat. no. 56]

Katherine Westphal,
Hawaiian Kitsch,
1978 [cat no. 56]

through them while Ed took photographs. These all turned into textiles [cat. no. 56]. I remember once in New York City at the Plaza Hotel – the fancy one – they were having a party for high-school kids, graduating seniors or something. On the stairs they had people dressed up as Snoopy and Mickey Mouse. Ed had his camera. He said he was going to take my picture, so I went up to Snoopy, and Snoopy got in the act, and we danced around on the stairs of the Plaza Hotel as Ed took pictures [cf. photos on pp. 10–11 and 30]....

I'm definitely a point-and-shoot photographer, and I have a very tiny automatic camera now. When I am pleased with a photograph, I have it enlarged up to eight by twelve. I have boxes of eight-by-twelve color photographs....

I will start something without a plan. I put something on a cloth, and then an idea hits. I look through the photographs and pull out the right thing and make a heat transfer and cut it up and put it down. Technically it's difficult. Once the heat transfer is down, no dye or color can be put underneath it....

I think this whole surprise thing has influenced everything I do. I never know exactly where anything is going; it just keeps growing, and I get an image of it in my mind and build on it.

SHIBORI AND OTHER JAPANESE METHODS   I was fascinated with hand techniques and the manipulation of resists, either wax or paste, and dye. Then I happened to see some *shibori* in a book. I made a little *shibori* piece. I didn't know how it was done, I just experimented. Several years later, Yoshiko Wada taught a class with Donna Larsen at Fiberworks Center for the Textile Arts [Berkeley] on *shibori* and other Japanese techniques and how to make indigo dyes and indigo baths. As with everything else, I became completely immersed in this. I progressed on to another class that Yoshiko taught on *katagami* and learned how to cut stencils out of mulberry paper.

PAPERMAKING   I learned how to make paper at Fiberworks from Nance O'Banion. I really enjoyed this. I was working with a very small screen frame and deckle that was nine inches. In order to learn how to pull these sheets of paper, I made paper every day, and our kitchen counters were filled with drying paper. There were all these stacks of little pieces of paper. I looked at all of them and decided that I could sew them together in the same way I did with cloth patches. These were decorative, but you could also wear them. I did a whole series of paper to wear, all kimono. I began combining them with cloth. I did a lot with photographs of Monet and photographs and drawings of flowers and Monet's garden [cat. no. 57], then I branched off into Chinese dragon skirts [cat. no. 58] and very large, oversized kimonos. Nobody ever wore them, they just hung them on sticks on walls. I expanded them. Everything got bigger: giant-sized garments.

27

BASKETRY   I was very conscious of all the baskets Ed was making. He was making all these containers, and there was a multitude of yarn and plastic and things left over from his projects. I am not very good in a technical sense at the making of three-dimensional forms by particular methods, as Ed was doing. I also wanted something that I could take with me and do wherever I was and that wouldn't require a lot of equipment. I decided that a crochet hook was the thing, and I began crocheting the plastic tubing and mylar that Ed had lying around into baskets, large-scale things that reflected light in many ways, almost like sequins [cat. nos. 48–51]. I also found in Ed's pile of stuff this synthetic raffia made of viscose rayon. He didn't want it anymore, so I started using the scraps [cat. nos. 59–60]. Later, I bought this raffia in a lot of colors and began making other forms. I learned how to control the crocheting to make a less-than-soft basket, and changed all these colors, using very slight variations of hue. It was wonderful to be able to work with linear elements, because I could use all these pure colors and crochet them together to get other colors. This really intrigued me.

Travel   THE UNIVERSITY had a wonderful sabbatical policy: every two-and-a-half years you could take a quarter off. Ed and I coordinated our sabbaticals so that we could travel together. There are textiles everywhere! This is wonderful for study proposals. We went to Peru with the World Craft Council in 1968. In 1970 we took a tour in Greece, then we went to Egypt. We were fascinated with Egypt, and then went on to Tunisia, Iran, Afghanistan, and India....

Everything I see sort of gets thrown together. It's almost as if my mind is an eggbeater, and I pick up little things and mix them togeth-

Ed Rossbach (standing, far right) and Katherine Westphal (standing, third from left) with their tour group before the Sphinx at Giza, Egypt, 1976 (photo courtesy of the artists). Westphal used this image in her quilt *New Treasures from Tutankhamun,* 1978 [cover and cat. no. 55]

er. Nothing is preconceived. I put something – a color, a shape – onto a textile or ground, and one thing leads to another. I rifle through the pile of scraps all around me on the table. I put things down, I take them off. I'm very much into collage. I move things around constantly, and when I finally decide it's right, it goes down. My work changes constantly; I never have a beginning idea. Very often, I don't know what it's all about until I'm through....

The large quilts with the pyramids, the camels, the dancing figures, and the workers around the edges are based on how I feel about Egypt, the connections I make between ancient Egypt and Egypt today, like the really touristy hype of having a camel named Ramses to ride to the Great Pyramid of Giza – this is all part of the thing [cover and cat. no. 55]. Another quilt is called *Hawaiian Kitsch* [cat. no. 56]. We went to Hawaii directly after we had been in Egypt. Egypt and Hawaii were so different that I put them both together. I gathered little sections of the newspapers from Hawaii with garish imagery in them: the Hilton Hotel girl with a rainbow over her head is in one of those quilts, plus camels and Heaven knows what....

Some of the gourds that I did in 1989 were a direct protest about what happened to the students in Tiananmen Square. I had been there earlier, seen all the posters, the masses of people moving around. Then, to see the street I had been on a year before all filled with tanks and people and banners recalled to me the 1968 disturbances at Berkeley. I had my color copier, and I clipped photographs from newspapers and various other sources. I began assembling the images, which I put on heat-transfer paper; then I transferred them onto rice paper and then laminated these onto gourds [cat. no. 68]. All the images of the Chinese people on the gourds are composites. I cut up the images and moved them around so

The Forbidden City, Tiananmen Square, Beijing, photographed by Katherine Westphal during a visit to China 1988 (photo courtesy of the artists)

nobody could be recognized except Chairman Mao. I wrote the little headlines from the newspapers and added them in. One of the headlines has flames coming up, symbolizing the destruction that was going on. I think that is the only violence that has ever found its way into my work, but I felt very strongly about it. I love China....

I like to travel, and you could mark off my life with travel signposts. You could also do it with dogs. I have had a whole string of dogs since 1950. Fifi, Pee Wee, Tyrone, Big Julie, Sam or Samurai, Molly, and now Susie Greasy Grass. I'm afraid that Susie Greasy Grass is the only blueblood of them all, and she is very difficult. She hasn't appeared in

Katherine with Snoopy on the steps of the Plaza Hotel, New York, 1992; and fiber sculpture of the artists' dog [cf. photo pp. 10–11], *Sam as Samurai* (photo collage by Katherine Westphal, courtesy of the artists)

art yet, but I'm sure she will. My dogs are part of my life – the playful side. They appear in my drawings, prints, and fiber sculpture: dogs speaking phonetic Japanese, eating sushi, or playing samurai warrior. Anything a human can do, a dog can do as well. They can also be just dogs.

Shared
Spaces

I THINK THE WORD is "cluttered." Ed and I have too much stuff, too many projects, too many ideas all going at once. You have to sort out and stake out an area that you're working in, and an area that you are thinking about. It's fascinating to see somebody else working and realize that people think and work in very different ways. From my viewpoint, what Ed does is very well thought out. He doesn't put things down until he understands the piece spatially and message-wise, perhaps. I work in just the opposite way. I never know where a piece is going. Things happen through intuition. There is no plan.

Another difference between us is that I tend to arrange things; I organize things; I put things in order on shelves; I stack up paper in order; and I label everything. Recently we had a leak in the roof over Ed's study. I went in to rescue his papers before they could get wet. I was just amazed. I carried them all into another room, and now he can't find things because they weren't in folders, they were just layered. Ed is like a geologist who knows how deep to look for what he wants to find. His studio area tends to be this way, also. In order to get space for something or other, I will take all his paint jars and move them onto a shelf and put them in a line. I know this drives him crazy, but

I have to order things that way, even though when I work, it's complete chaos. Ed has chaos around him, but his methods and his work are very orderly. It is a crazy mixture....

It's fascinating to watch someone who is able to take string, or old newspapers, or garbage, and somehow create wonderful three-dimensional forms with them. Ed is very, very good at creating three-dimensional forms with materials that I would think had no possibilities. What is interesting to me is that when I somehow get hold of the cast-off materials and try to do something with them, although I am using the same materials, my things are not structural; they are dizzy, going in all directions. I'm using the same materials in very different ways. Basically, we both are using color, paint, brushes, sticks, and strings, but it comes out differently with each person who is manipulating these things....

Ed and I talk constantly about art in general and about other people's work: we evaluate what they think they're doing, but we tend pretty much not to invade each other's territory. It's a tricky situation. After all, we're both equals – one isn't the teacher and one the learner. We learn tremendous amounts from each other, from the other person's perceptions. When we go to an exhibit, we don't talk about it while we're seeing it, but when we get back to the hotel we talk about it, and in the same room I've seen something very different from what he has seen. You almost have to go back and take another look to see what this was. Very often there are things that we both like very, very much. We just fasten on the same object. Why this is, I don't know.

Katherine Westphal in the two artists' shared studio, 1992 (photo courtesy of the artists)

Selected quotes assembled and edited by Paul J. Smith for the following format; excerpted from "Charles Edmund Rossbach, Artist, Mentor, Professor, Writer," an oral history conducted in 1983 by Harriet Nathan, Regional Oral History Office, The Bancroft Library, University of California, Berkeley, 1987. (Bracketed numbers refer to pages of the oral history transcription.)

ED ROSSBACH

Formative Years

GRANDMOTHER'S TATTING   My grandmother used to tat...When you talked to her, she was sitting there tatting away. She would ride in the car, and she was tatting all the time. [3]

She would give these handkerchiefs for Christmas and send them in envelopes to various people that she knew. I think maybe it was my first contact with textiles as being valuable beyond themselves. I think we knew at the time that these were old-fashioned and people didn't want little edgings on handkerchiefs anymore, and yet, you valued them because she had done them. I think it is still part of my feeling about textiles, that the work is very important to this thing and you are aware that somebody made this. [4]

I always wondered about...all this tatting that she did. She would do a little row that had three little drops. She never varied these things....I would do two inches of that stuff, and then I would be experimenting with the next thing to see how I could do it, but she never changed the form or the thread that she was using. She never turned it into little rounds or made inserts or did anything that you could do with patterns. She always did the same thing. [4]

Not so long ago I learned to tat. I got a book and learned how to do it. I have some things I have made, and it just seemed very amusing to me to learn how to do it. This is all part of the amusement of those things. I mean what an absurd thing; I am an old man sitting here learning how to tat from a book! It's the absurdity...that's the fun of it. [4–5]

SISTERS' PASTIMES   My sisters took to making patchwork quilts, and it seemed like we always had patchwork quilts spread out in the basement on stretchers. The family would all sit down there quilting. [9] They just sewed for their hope chests and that sort of thing, and those were beautiful quilts. [9] Sometimes I would read to them. There were clear ideas of what was permitted and what was all right, but I was terribly interested in it, and I still am. [9]

My sisters did this embroidery. They were doing it all of the time. They were always knitting...but this was all women's work. I have thought since that this was like a primitive society where the distinction is made that women do certain things and men do certain things. In certain societies women do the baskets, and the men don't do the baskets, but the men know how to do it. They watch this thing, and they understand it completely, but they don't do it, and this was how this was with all of this embroidery and stuff which my sisters did. I did not do it, of course. [6]

My sister Ruth had bought a loom. It was available somewhere, a secondhand loom, and she brought it home. We had it down in our basement for a while; it was a very bad loom. I wove a little on it. I wove more than she ever did on the thing, but it was just such a bad loom. [12]

Since that early time I have felt uncomfortable doing anything like sewing, darning, appliquéing, embroidering. I avoid them in my own work as somehow not appropriate activity for a man – knitting, also – any of these textile techniques that my sisters did. [7]

I realize that when I was a child I was very solitary (as I still am) and that I devoted much time to constructing. I had an Erector Set, a Meccano Set, Tinker Toys, and Lincoln Logs. I spent quantities of time amusing myself building: not wildly elaborate structures like those in the catalogues, but simple constructions, over and over. I feel that this interest is incorporated in my textiles. [7]

THIS WAS A REMARKABLE high school at that time. When I think back on it and what we did in English and so on, my God, you were reading the best that had been written [Kate Smith was Rossbach's English teacher at Lyons Township High School]. Well, I don't think they all read Shakespeare to the extent we did in high school. It's just a wonder. I am so glad I went to that particular school. [11]

Edith Blaisdell Murphy was the art teacher. [10] She was interested in theater, and there was what we called an All Arts Klub, and we used to give a play every year. [11] She would take us to Chicago, and we would go to the Art Institute. We did everything in Chicago with this art teacher, and this was very wonderful. [12]

Lyons Township High School

AT THE END OF THE DEPRESSION, we [Ed and his sisters] got in the car and drove down to the fair at Treasure Island in California and saw the decorative arts exhibit that Dorothy Liebes had installed there. I didn't know anything about Dorothy Liebes, naturally. I saw these contemporary textiles and weaving and wrote in my diary that I would like to learn how to weave so that I could weave upholstery. [4]

Visiting the Golden Gate International Exposition, San Francisco 1940

IN WEAVING I WAS NOT a typical Cranbrook student. I would be surprised if Marianne Strengell, the teacher, even remembers who I was. I was beginning to be sort of a maverick there before I got through. For a while, I was just going along, you know, doing what everybody else was doing, and gradually I began to see possibilities in this thing that were going off in other directions which didn't exactly please her. [80]

Cranbrook Academy of Art

Teaching

Sᴏᴍᴇʜᴏᴡ ᴛʜᴇ ʏᴏᴜɴɢ ᴘᴇᴏᴘʟᴇ that one deals with...seem so knowledgeable and so experienced...this has been my experience ever since I started teaching. From the time I was teaching seventh grade, I felt the children were more knowledgeable than I was, and they *were*! [19]

I think I have gone through the whole of my own life feeling that way. I don't know enough, I haven't experienced enough. [19]

When I came to Berkeley, I had such a limited knowledge of textile techniques...the students knew so much more than I did....there would be these displays in the hall...and the students would be there figuring out these things, whether this was double cloth, triple cloth, whether this was – well, whatever. I didn't know these things myself, and here I was teaching these students. I had to learn. I had to learn fast. [88]

I think this has influenced my teaching in a way, because I have tended to let the students take the lead, which I approve of. I think that's okay....I feel that they are more into things than I am, more into what is happening and what is going to happen and so on. I just sort of follow along and look at this in wonderment. [19]

I think sometimes when teaching, you have students who are obviously influenced very directly by somebody, and you feel they have almost lifted a photograph out of a book. You've seen pieces where you know where it came from. And that's okay. I mean, why not? [126]

I think the whole history of textiles has been repeating and repeating; and nothing is ever repeated exactly as it has been before [cat. nos. 3, 5, 8–9]. I think it's important that they know where the influence came from....It's really important to know what you have been influenced by, if possible, and I like the idea of giving credit to it, to the person or thing. [126]

Ed Rossbach at Berkeley, 1974
(photo courtesy of the artists)

[Take] Anni Albers, for instance; her work has been reworked a thousand times. You get the idea of this thing and rework it. I think that's great. You might just call it "Homage to Anni Albers." Why not? I mean, it was an interesting intellectual problem for her, and it is for a student, too, or for anyone. [126]

Marcel Proust

Pʀᴏᴜsᴛ ʜᴀs ᴀ ᴛʀᴇᴍᴇɴᴅᴏᴜs impact for me. He seems to be reaching the same conclusions [that I have], which I read in many ways, and it's very comforting to have Proust reach these conclusions. It seems to make things all right, somehow – the fluidity of everything. What was up is down. What is important is unimportant....his insights into the way the world goes. Sometimes you read along, and

34

you don't even know that you are being impressed by these insights; then you think about them later, and it all adds up to this big, mind-blowing sort of thing. [94]

...And the sensitivity, of course, to everything...certainly make[s] you look at the French landscape differently, from having read Proust. [94]

We were on the Normandy coast and in Brittany last year [1982], and now that I'm reading Proust again, why, no other descriptions of sky and the beach can compare. You just see things more perceptively from having read Proust. [94]

It is the same thing if you look at a painting by Van Gogh and then you go through Van Gogh country, and it all looks like Van Gogh, or Cézanne, or whatever. Everything looks like Proust, and you know he is speaking truth. [94]

I THINK THE ESSENCE of me in my work is trying to understand. *Trying to* You don't have to understand everything, and sometimes it drives *Understand* Katherine crazy....You try these techniques, and what are they? What do they do? What's the difference?...You explore...how they've been used historically. Then, you try to understand how they have meaning for you or your time: what they look like done in plastic. [90]

I look at certain things that I did many years ago, and I like them very much. I think from this vantage point of time, you see all the directions, this Y-effect that they talk about – that you might have done this, or you might have done that – and you see seeds of possibilities in your early work that for some reason or other you didn't pursue. I think it is interesting. [86]

I did a very complicated thing. It was netting with pile [cat. no. 9]. You do these things, and who is your audience? Who is going to know that you've done netting with pile? Maybe it's not important that anybody should know that this is netting with pile. I did scaffolding textiles according to a Peruvian technique [cat. nos. 3, 5]. Well, then it just turns out to be a textile. Who knows that you scaffolded this thing? It couldn't be achieved any other way, but who knows enough about textiles to know that it couldn't be achieved any other way? [91]

I wish [that] as I grow older, my work would get more playful. I read a review of a Dubuffet exhibit and how his work is changing as he grows into old age. Somehow it didn't occur to me particularly that things should change as you move into these different time periods of your life, and I thought, "Why can't I be more playful at this point in my life and do more exactly what I believe in?" [71]

I like things to be so simple and so innocent and so direct that you just look at it and you think, "A child could do that; I mean, think of an adult doing that. What's in it?" And this is what I believe in, but I can't allow myself to do those things or offer them for exhibition very much, because they just don't seem enough and I don't feel that people understand what I am doing. I want to be understood somehow, and I don't particularly like...to be rebuffed. [71]

IT SEEMED THAT I WAS FLITTING from one thing to the next in a way that...I wouldn't really admire in someone else. It looks kind of flighty, but it was all okay for me. There wasn't a consistency of using the same technique, but the consistency came, I think, through various techniques. I felt the same way about materials. I wanted to try everything. [89]

[When I read about] these techniques, I had to try them myself. I couldn't understand the techniques unless I really did them myself. I would do these techniques, and then I felt it was important to try...a piece of, say, knitting, or one piece of knotless netting, or whatever it would be, something like that. I did a lot of knotless netting, actually. I liked that. [89]

IKATS   A long time ago I was working on ikats, and I was taking these bundles of yarn and tying them to resist the dye. Each bundle was tied at a different interval, so that some of them had the intervals very fast, some of them had them very slow, and then I arranged all

Ed Rossbach tying ikat warp threads on the porch of the studio, Berkeley, 1960 (photo courtesy of the artists)

these bundles into a warp and wove them, so that you had these stripes with these intervals of ikats going up, all at different rates [cat. no. 10]. I felt that there was a "time" quality to them...some moving fast and some moving slowly. It reminded me of a ballet that I had seen, where all these figures were moving across the stage, and some were walking very slowly, and some were moving very rapidly, and this whole thing was going on at once. I tried to get that in a textile. Well, I was the only one who had the slightest conception of what I was trying to do. I don't know if it was important...but at least that's what I was trying to do. [98]

RAFFIA   Some years ago I did a large raffia piece. It was done on a frame, which I expected to be part of it. When I had the thing finished, the tension on this raffia was so strong that it pulled the frame in, and there was no way that I could force that frame out again. The thing had an awkward shape, which I didn't like; so I made this bold decision that I would just cut this thing off the frame, no matter what happened. You know, it was like risking all, really, because I'd worked so long on this thing...then I was just going to take a knife and cut this off, which I did; and it changed the thing very much....I liked it, and I was pleased that I had done this. This was when we were sending [work] to the *Triennale* in Milan. I was trying to decide what I would send, and Katherine said, "Send that!" – I couldn't imagine sending that now; it looks very conventional – so I sent it...then subsequently the Museum of Modern Art bought it. They put it back on a frame, which is amusing to me, and, of course, now the frame is all right, because they had a new frame and the tension wasn't as it had been...theoretically they had it the way I originally thought of it. [81]

MICKEY MOUSE   I use Mickey Mouse as an image very frequently   *Imagery*
in my work [cat. nos. 15, 44], almost because these things require
images. If you're doing knotless netting, you
need an image; or [rather] I want an image.
What image do you put in nowadays? [In
other] times the images were there for you,
certain religious images...now, in our culture, what images do you put in?...You put in
Mickey Mouse, and it's a statement about
that....I like Mickey Mouse. I think it's [also]
partly...a defensive attitude on my part...
[People] refer to the classes that you teach as
Mickey Mouse classes, and everything is just
dismissed..."It's Mickey Mouse." Somehow
this is very damaging, so I put a Mickey
Mouse on baskets and the most elaborate textiles. I wove Mickey Mouse in double damask.
I did him in ikats. I've done a lot of Mickey
Mouses. [91]

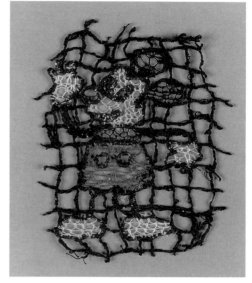

Ed Rossbach
Mickey Mouse Lace, 1971 [cat no. 15]

PETE ROSE   When they were interviewing me on Canadian Broadcasting and I was holding some of these baskets with images on them, they said, "Why did you use the imagery of this baseball player, Pete Rose?" Well, I think if I were being absolutely honest, I would just say, "I happened to see this thing in a magazine. It was the right size. I liked it. For some reason it spoke to me. I just liked it as an image, and I put it on the basket." That doesn't persuade anybody; so you have to think of some reason that will be more persuasive. Of course, Pete Rose has been in these television ads of someone with gray hair who is competing in a youth-oriented society...he uses some hair tonic, and his hair gets darker again, so he is [looking like] a young man. It is this older man in a youth-oriented society, surviving. Well, it's very persuasive, so [I say] that's why I used Pete Rose and [also] I like the name Rose. I like the idea of a Rose basket, but that really had nothing to do with why I used it. It was lying around here, and I saved it; but I don't know anything about Pete Rose, and I don't care anything about baseball...when I put [on] the heat transfer, things were reversed, so that if he were a right-handed batter, he turned out to be a left-handed batter. I don't know if he is right- or left-handed. [136–137]

JOHN TRAVOLTA   I used a heat-transfer image of John Travolta [cat. no. 20]. Well, why did I use Travolta? I used Travolta because I suddenly wanted to put an image on this piece of cloth. I just felt this had to have an image, and in the paper that day there was a picture of John Travolta which was the right size, and I colored it and made a heat transfer of it and put it on. I suppose someone would say, "Well, there, you may not know why you put it on, but there was a reason why you put it on." Well, I don't know. Certainly I've never thought much about John Travolta, except that I saw him on the airplane in that movie – *Saturday Night Fever*. I just thought the man was wonderfully lively, energetic, just marvelous, and I like this quality, this youth, so sometimes I say that's why I put it on there, but it was almost like choosing Mickey Mouse. It's just Mickey Mouse. [137]

Coptic Textiles

W E WENT TO EGYPT, and I thought it would be fun when we were in Cairo to buy a Coptic textile, so we found an antique...store, and indeed they had Coptic textiles. They dragged out this enormous stack of Coptic textiles, and we went through them one at a time. We couldn't believe that there are so many Coptic textiles in existence and so beautiful, so we bought one. [75]

Anyway, I was intrigued by the idea of why these little, tiny Coptic figures are so expressive, how they achieve this expressiveness, what there is about them that is so good. I found out that the De Young Museum [M. H. De Young Memorial Museum, San Francisco] had a collection of some Coptic textiles that were given to them. So I borrowed these Coptic textiles, and I had them photographed under magnification so that I could blow these things up big and look at the structure of the thing, and see what the images would look like large, whether they lost the quality large, or what happened to them. Then, I began to use these images and made them enormous. [75]

I did this little Coptic head in a pile [technique]. It didn't look anything like a Coptic head at all, but it did look like the woman across the street...the sort of look that she had when she would get up in the morning and pick up her paper...in her bathrobe. Her name was Mrs. Cross, and so I called this textile *Early Cross* [cat. no. 9]. It just delights me to think that anyone might try to find a religious significance [in it]. [91]

Ed Rossbach creating a Coptic-style textile at the drawloom in the weaving studio, University of California, Berkeley, during the 1970s (photo courtesy of the artists)

Art Out of Trash

I THINK I WAS MAKING ART out of trash quite a while ago, but not in the same flamboyant way that people are doing it now. It was very restrained and almost down-pedaling the fact that this was made out of trash...out of old plastic boxes. I was cutting them up and transforming them into new material that I then wove. It didn't have the quality of trash necessarily, which I think a lot of this stuff does, when they just assemble a lot of stuff – like in Simon's towers, where he takes broken pottery and all this stuff and just assembles it. You look at it, and you know at once that this is just a big bunch of junk which has been assembled; but mine didn't have that quality. [95]

Selected quotes from an interview conducted by Paul J. Smith, April 9–11, 1997

Katherine has a fresh spontaneity when she works that is fun to watch. People should be interested in watching her. She's kind of a showman. I am not. *Working Alongside Katherine*

She has an enormous talent for drawing. It just flows. I agonize over things. I wonder what in the world I think I am doing.

It's been kind of interesting and stimulating to work in conjunction with Katherine. People ask, "How do you collaborate?" We don't collaborate; that's the point. We could both be working in the same studio, and we'd have no apparent influence on each other; but of course there is an influence there. Finally, when I see things at the end of a long period, I don't know whether I made it or Katherine made it, and that's kind of unnerving. I don't approve of it and so on, but there it is.

Talking about Katherine's work, I more than ever feel it's of wonderful quality, and I wonder why she hasn't been more successful; then I wonder what I mean by "success." Well, I don't know. I suppose it means something different to everybody. I have sort of an idea of what I think success is, and in that way I think I have been more successful than she has. It doesn't mean that my work is any better or worse or anything else. Success is just a recognition that you exist. We all can't have something in the Museum of Modern Art, but we would like to. You want someone to respond to your work, because making it is really exposing yourself.

Biographical Information: Katherine Westphal and Ed Rossbach

COMPILED BY PAUL J. SMITH

KATHERINE WESTPHAL

1919
Born January 2 in Los Angeles to Emma and Leo Westphal

1926–32
Attends Alexandria Elementary School, Los Angeles

1932–34
Attends Virgil Junior High School, Los Angeles

1934–37
Attends Fairfax High School, Los Angeles

1937–41
Attends Los Angeles City College and graduates with Associate of Arts degree

1941–43
Attends University of California, Berkeley (UCB), where she studies painting with Worth Ryder and receives BA and MA degrees

1943
Awarded the James Phelan Traveling Scholarship in fall and travels in Mexico for three months, visiting the studios of muralists and meeting David Siqueiros and Diego Rivera

1943–44
Takes weaving classes with Lea Miller in Decorative Art Department at UCB

1944
Takes summer jewelry workshop with Ruth Pennington at UCB

1945
Accepts one-year teaching position (art) at University of Wyoming, Laramie

1946–50
Teaches two-dimensional design and drawing in the Art Department at the University of Washington, Seattle

1947
Meets Ed Rossbach in Seattle

1950
Marries Ed Rossbach in Seattle, then moves to Berkeley, where Ed has accepted a teaching position at UCB

1951
Studies textile surface design with Mary Dumas at UCB

1951–58
Designs printed textiles for Perspectives, Inc., New York, through agent Frederick Karoly

1952
Takes class in costume and textile history with Anna Gayton at UCB

1953–55
Studies ceramics with Edith Heath and Hal Reiger at California College of Arts and Crafts, Oakland

1956–57
Spends nine months in Europe with Ed on his sabbatical leave

1960
Spends one month in Spain and Morocco with Ed

1961
Begins making quilted wall hangings

1964
Represented in USA exhibit at Milan *Triennale*

1966
Accepts teaching position in design in the Department of Applied Behavior Science, College of Agriculture, University of California, Davis (UCD)

Exhibits with Ed at American Craft Council's Museum West, San Francisco

1968
Exhibits with Ed at American Craft Council's Museum of Contemporary Crafts, New York

Becomes associate professor at UCD

1969
Represented in *OBJECTS: USA, The Johnson Collection of Contemporary Crafts*, organized by the Smithsonian Institution, Washington, D.C.; national and international tour

1970
Spends two months in Greece, Egypt, India, and Italy with Ed

1975
Gives lecture/workshop at Fiberworks
Center for the Textile Arts, Berkeley

Made full professor at UCD

1977
Receives National Endowment for the
Arts fellowship

1978
Represented in exhibition *American
Crafts at the Vatican*, Rome

1979
Retires as Professor of Design Emeritus
at UCD

Travels to Indonesia

Becomes a Fellow of the American
Craft Council

*Dragons and Other Creatures – Looking
at Chinese Embroidery* published by
Lancaster-Miller Publishing

1980
Presents "Wearable Art" program at
World Craft Council conference in
Vienna

1980–81
Artist in Residence (Jacquard program),
Rhode Island School of Design,
Providence

1984
One-person exhibition, *Paper to Wear*,
San Francisco Craft and Folk Art
Museum

1985
Artist in Residence (paper), Southwest
Craft Center, San Antonio

1988
Exhibition, *Wearable Furniture*, Design
Gallery, UCD

1989
Alumni Citation for Excellence, UCD

PRESENTLY WORKS IN STUDIO
SHARED WITH ED IN BERKELEY

ED ROSSBACH
(Charles Edmund Rossbach)

1914
Born January 2 in Edison Park, Illinois
(near Chicago), to Anna and Charles
Rossbach

1922
Moves with parents and sisters Doris,
Ruth, and Jane to Seattle

1924
Moves with family to Tacoma

1928
Moves with family back to Chicago area
and attends Lyons Township High
School, LaGrange

1930–40
Observes quilting being done by aunts
and sisters and does a little weaving on
small second-hand loom acquired by
sister

1931
Family settles permanently in Seattle

Takes weaving class at Broadway Night
School

1932
Becomes interested in making marionettes and performs with sister in
churches and schools

1938
Attends University of Washington,
Seattle, but after two semesters takes a
six-month civil service job in Spokane

Returns to the University on Phi Beta
Kappa Scholarship and studies with
Amédée Ozenfant and Johannes
Molzahn

Making Marionettes published by
Harcourt, Brace & Co., New York

1940
Receives BA degree in Painting and
Design at University of Washington,
Seattle, graduating Phi Beta Kappa and
magna cum laude

Makes trip with sisters to San Francisco
to see the Golden Gate International
Exposition, where decorative arts exhibit
organized by Dorothy Liebes motivates
his interest in weaving

Receives Romette Stevens Scholarship
to attend Columbia University, New
York, where Belle Boas, supervisor of
student teachers, is an important
influence

1941
Receives MA degree in art education
from Columbia University, New York

Returns to Seattle to accept first teaching position: seventh grade in Puyallup
Junior High School (near Seattle)

1942
Enlists in US Army and joins Signal
Core Alaska Communication System

1945
Assigned one-year tour of duty in Adak,
Aleutian Islands, where he is inspired
by the beauty of the country and its
natural grasses to make baskets from
grasses and to draw landscapes

1946
After release from US Army, attends
Cranbrook Academy of Art, Bloomfield
Hills, under GI Bill and studies ceram-
ics with Maija Grotell and textiles with
Marianne Strengell

1947
Receives MFA degree from Cranbrook
Academy of Art, Bloomfield Hills

Returns to Seattle to accept teaching
position at the University of Washington
in two departments: Art and Home
Economics

Meets Katherine Westphal, who is
teaching design and illustration in the
same program

1949
Lea Miller, former teacher in Seattle
and head of weaving at University of
California, Berkeley (UCB), extends invi-
tation to conduct summer class at UCB
with the possibility of becoming full-
time faculty

1950
Marries Katherine Westphal in Seattle

Winfield Scott Wellington, Chairman of
Decorative Art Department, UCB,
arranges meeting with Dorothy Liebes
at her San Francisco studio

Accepts position of Assistant Professor
of Design at UCB in fall

1951–58
Designs printed textiles for
Perspectives, Inc., New York, through
agent Frederick Karoly

1950–60
Takes evening ceramic classes at
California College of Arts and Crafts,
Oakland

1956
Made associate professor at UCB

1956–57
Spends nine months in Europe on sabbatical leave with Katherine

1958
Represented in exhibit at US Pavilion,
Brussels World Fair

1960
Spends one month in Spain and
Morocco with Katherine

1963
Made full professor at UCB

1964
Represented in USA exhibit at Milan
Triennale

1966
Exhibits with Katherine at American
Craft Council's Museum West, San
Francisco

1968
Exhibits with Katherine at American
Craft Council's Museum of
Contemporary Crafts, New York

1969
Represented in exhibition Wall Hangings,
Museum of Modern Art, New York

Represented in OBJECTS: USA, The
Johnson Collection of Contemporary Crafts,
organized by the Smithsonian
Institution, Washington, D.C.; national
and international tour

1970
Spends two months in Greece, Egypt,
India, and Italy with Katherine

1973
Baskets as Textile Art published by Van
Nostrand Reinhold Company, New York

1975
Decorative Art Department merged
with College of Environmental Design
to become Program of Visual Design,
which is phased out in the next few
years at UCB

Becomes a Fellow of the American
Craft Council

1976
The New Basketry published by Van
Nostrand Reinhold Company, New York

1977
Receives National Endowment for the
Arts fellowship

1978
Represented in exhibition American
Crafts at the Vatican, Rome

1979
Retires as Professor Emeritus, UCB

1980
The Art of Paisley published by Van
Nostrand Reinhold Company, New York

1980–81
Artist in Residence (Jacquard program),
Rhode Island School of Design,
Providence

1985
Honored as a "Living Treasure of
California" by Creative Arts League,
Sacramento

1986
The Nature of Basketry published by
Schiffer Publishing, Exton, Pennsylvania

1990
Retrospective exhibition organized by
the Textile Museum, Washington, D.C.,
with catalogue, ED ROSSBACH: 40
Years of Exploration and Innovation in
Fiber Art

Honored by the American Craft Council
with a Gold Medal for highest achieve-
ment in craftsmanship

PRESENTLY WORKS IN STUDIO
SHARED WITH KATHERINE IN
BERKELEY

Checklist of the Exhibition

S USAN H AY

All works are on loan from Daphne Farago.
Height precedes width precedes depth in all measurements.

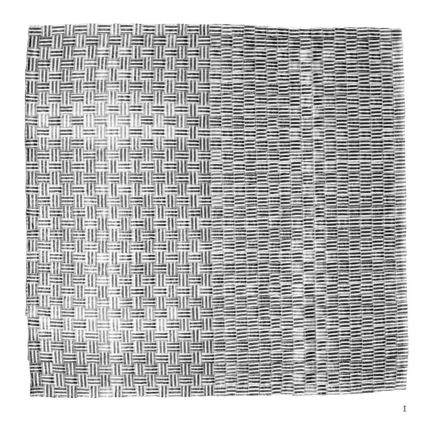

1
ED ROSSBACH
*Reconstituted Commercial
Textile*, 1960
Polyethylene film tubing,
commercial cotton fabric
with printed stripe; plaited,
tie-dyed, discharged
35½ × 35 inches

2
ED ROSSBACH
Homage to John Glenn, 1962
Cotton; double-weave
pick-up
48¼ × 29½ inches

3
ED ROSSBACH
Mont Saint Michel, 1964
Raffia, synthetic raffia; plain
weave, interlocked discontinuous warps and wefts
18 × 8½ inches

3

2

6, 4

5

4
ED ROSSBACH
Hornet's Nest, 1964
Raffia, synthetic raffia, sisal,
gesso; coiled
9¼ × 11¾ × 10⅛ inches

5
ED ROSSBACH
Delta, 1964
Raffia, cotton; plain-weave,
interlocked discontinuous
warps and wefts
10¼ × 19 inches

6
ED ROSSBACH
Looped Cylinder Basket, 1964
Rattan; looped
13 × 7½ × 8½ inches

7
ED ROSSBACH
*Old Moon in New Moon's
Arms*, 1965
Bast fiber, plastic tubing;
macramé
16 × 14½ × 2¾ inches

7

8

9

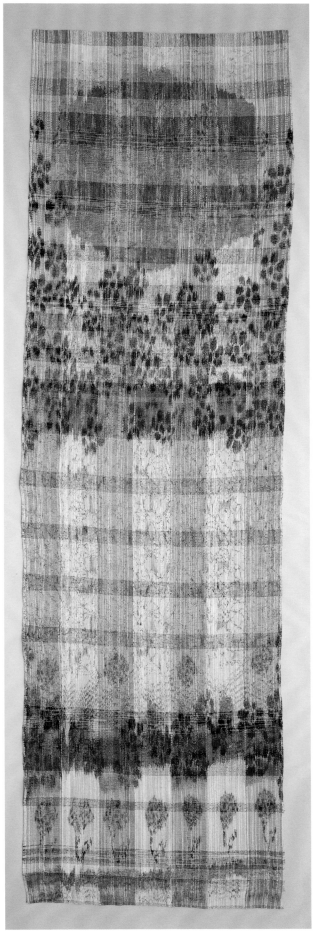

8
ED ROSSBACH
Double-Cloth Experiment,
1966
Cotton; double cloth
7 × 6⅛ inches

9
ED ROSSBACH
Early Cross, 1967
Wool, cotton; knotted
netting with pile
13 × 12 inches

10
ED ROSSBACH
Small Hanging with Flowers,
1968
Cotton; warp ikat
77 × 23 inches

10

11
Ed Rossbach
World Egg, 1969
Sisal, jute, polyethylene film
tubing; macramé
28½ × 26 inches

12
Ed Rossbach
Rag Tassel, 1970
Cotton, sticks, duct tape;
plaited, tied, taped
33 × 14¾ inches

13
Ed Rossbach
Layered Mesh, 1970
Polyethylene garbage bags;
looped
34½ × 37 inches

12

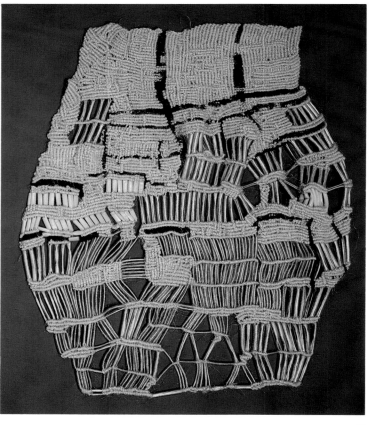

11

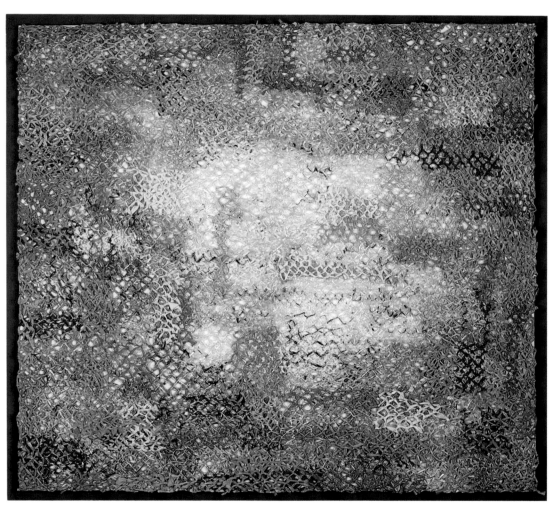

13

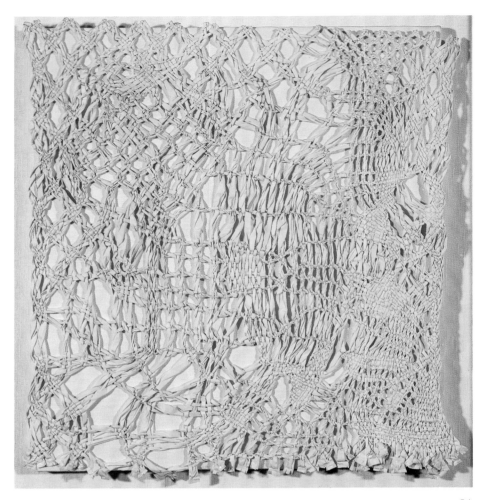

14

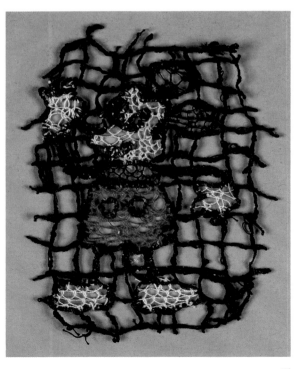

15

14
ED ROSSBACH
Tagging-Tape Lace, 1970
Polyethylene; bobbin lace
18½ × 17 inches

15
ED ROSSBACH
Mickey Mouse Lace, 1971
Cotton; needle lace
3½ × 3 inches

16
ED ROSSBACH
Cairn, 1973
Cotton tape, paper backing;
diagonally plaited, silk-
screened
19½ × 11 × 8 inches

16

17

17
ED ROSSBACH
Rag Basket, 1973
Commercial fabric,
corrugated paper; diagonally
plaited, silk-screened
8½ × 11¼ × 11 inches

18
ED ROSSBACH
Coiled Newspaper Basket, 1974
Newspaper, polyethylene
film tubing, cotton string;
coiled
6 × 8 inches (diam.)

19
ED ROSSBACH
Drop Cloth, 1975
Plastic-coated paper, cotton;
double-layer diagonally
plaited, stuffed
63½ × 46½ inches

18

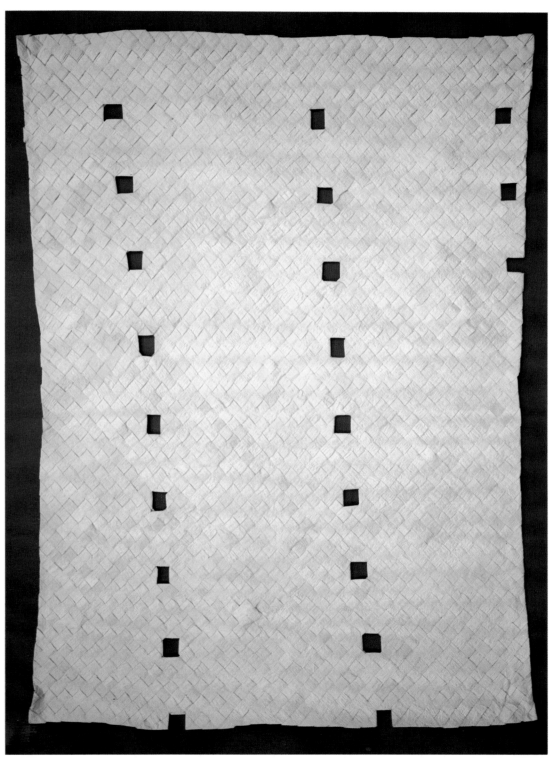

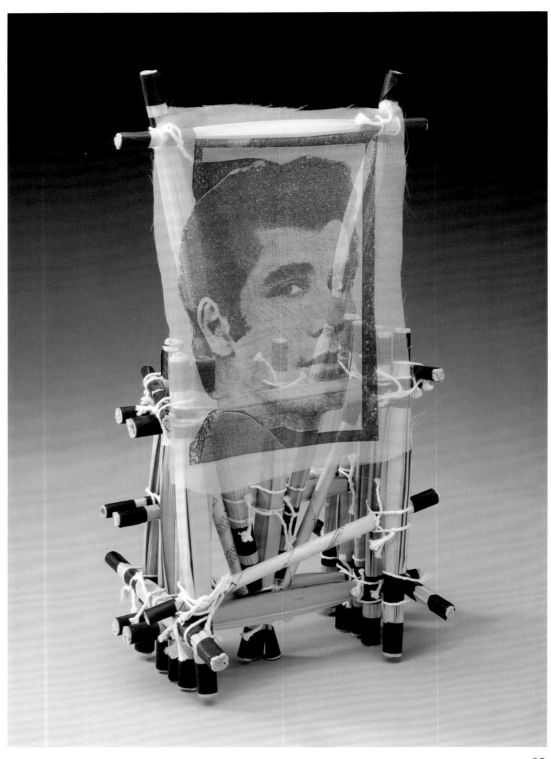

20
ED ROSSBACH
John Travolta, 1978
Reeds, cotton twine,
commercial silk organza,
electrical tape, newspaper;
tied, color-photocopy heat-
transfer
16 × 9 × 7 inches

21
ED ROSSBACH
Cylindrical Vessel, 1979
Cotton; plaited
7¾ × 4½ inches (diam.)

22
ED ROSSBACH
Patterned Plaiting, 1981
Foil; diagonally plaited
3½ × 3½ inches (diam.)

23
ED ROSSBACH
Basic Basket, 1981
Foil; diagonally plaited
5¼ × 3½ inches (diam.)

24
ED ROSSBACH
Carosol, 1981
Foil; diagonally plaited
4⅛ × 3⅓ inches (diam.)

25
ED ROSSBACH
Secret of Life, 1981
Foil, cotton; plaited
6¾ × 6¼ inches (diam.)

21

22, 23, 25, 24

26

26
ED ROSSBACH
Red Elephant, 1982
Ash splints, paper; plaited,
painted
4¼ × 6 inches (diam.)

27
ED ROSSBACH
Progression, 1983
Ash splints, rice paper;
diagonally plaited, painted
21 × 12 inches (diam.)

28
ED ROSSBACH
Eagle's Nest, 1984
Twigs, raffia, corrugated
cardboard, newspaper; tied
construction, painted
15½ × 16 × 16 inches

29
ED ROSSBACH
Purple Box, 1985
Ash splints, commercial
fabric, newspaper, acrylic
paint, twine; plaited, tied
9 × 11 × 6⅝ inches

27

28

29

30
ED ROSSBACH
Croissants, 1987
Commercial cardboard
packaging; spray-painted,
stapled
16 × 8 inches (diam.)

31
ED ROSSBACH
Mummies Room, 1987
Cardboard, paper; photocopy
heat-transfer, spray-painted,
stapled
7⅝ × 8 × 7¾ inches

32
ED ROSSBACH
Poetry of Grasslands, 1987
Coated cardboard, paper;
photocopy heat-transfer,
spray-painted, stapled
8½ × 8 inches (diam.)

33
ED ROSSBACH
Dark Indian, 1987
Mexican bark paper, palm
leaves, commercial cotton
fabric; heat-transfer, folded,
stapled
3¼ × 9⅜ inches (diam.)

34
ED ROSSBACH
Good Omen, 1988–90
Bark, cotton tassels,
imitation fur, corn husks;
folded, stapled
8¾ × 10 inches (diam.)

30

33

34

31, 32

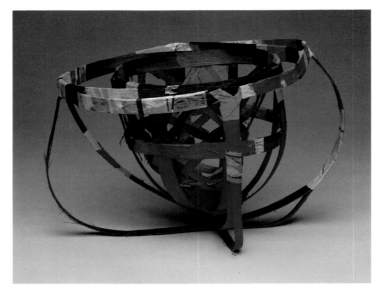

35

36

38

35
ED ROSSBACH
Suspended Color, 1988
Willow, cotton, tape; bent,
woven, stapled, taped,
painted
7¼ × 11 × 9 inches

36
ED ROSSBACH
Old Corral, 1989
Ash splints, paper, rawhide,
commercial cotton fabric,
twigs; plaited, tied, silk-
screened
9½ × 7¾ × 7¾ inches

37
ED ROSSBACH
Lebanon, 1989
Cardboard, paper; color-
photocopy heat-transfer,
stapled
14½ × 6 inches (diam.)

38
ED ROSSBACH
Iridescent Cubic Basket, 1990
Plastic; origami
5¾ × 4¾ × 4¾ inches

39
ED ROSSBACH
Upright Column, 1991
Ash splints, paper; plaited,
color-photocopy heat-transfer,
overpainted
21 × 5 × 5 inches

37

39

40

41

40
ED ROSSBACH
The Great Buffalo Spirit, 1991
Ash splints, paper, twine;
plaited, tied, color-photocopy
heat-transfer
10 × 8¼ × 9 inches

41
ED ROSSBACH
Greek Soap, 1992
Ash splints, paper; plaiting,
pen-and-ink drawing
12 × 9½ × 7 inches

42
ED ROSSBACH
The Very Small Moon, 1992
Ash splints, paper, palm
fronds; plaited, tied,
pen-and-ink lettering
4½ × 10 × 10 inches

43
ED ROSSBACH
Athene, 1992
Paper, bark; plaited, heat-
transfer, pen-and-ink
drawing
11 × 11 inches (diam.)

42

43

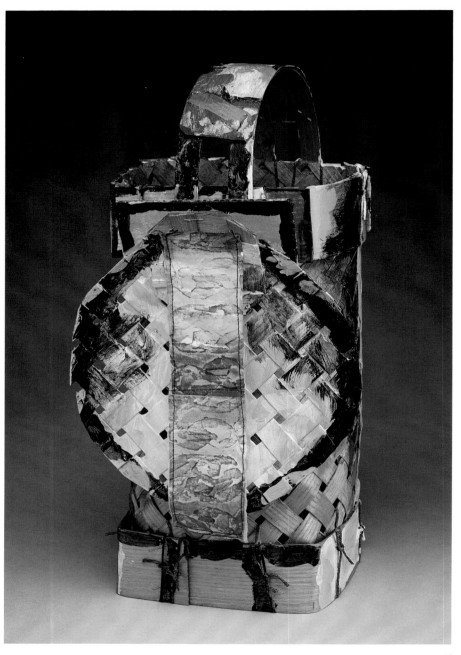

45

44
ED ROSSBACH
Reconstruction, 1992
Ash splints, paper; plaited,
felt-tipped-pen and pen-
and-ink drawing
7¾ × 10½ × 10½ inches

45
ED ROSSBACH
Egg Roll, Phase II, 1993–95
Ash splints, paper, twine;
plaited, heat-transfer,
painted, tied
14½ × 7¾ × 7½ inches

46
ED ROSSBACH
To Measure the Moon, 1994
Ash splints, paper; plaited,
color-photocopy heat-
transfer, stapled
13 × 10 × 9 inches

46

44

47

48, 49, 51, 50

47
KATHERINE WESTPHAL
Peruvian Monkeys, 1967
Cotton; quilted, embroi-
dered, batiked, block-printed
19¼ × 19¾ inches

48
KATHERINE WESTPHAL
Brunhilde, 1974
Foil; crocheted
8¼ × 7 × 6 inches

49
KATHERINE WESTPHAL
Gerhilde, 1974
Foil; crocheted
4½ × 4½ × 5¼ inches

50
KATHERINE WESTPHAL
Ortlinde, 1974
Foil; crocheted
6 × 7 × 6½ inches

51
KATHERINE WESTPHAL
Rossweisse, 1974
Foil; crocheted
13 × 5 × 5½ inches

52
KATHERINE WESTPHAL
Martha, 1975
Polyester tubing; crocheted
6½ × 8¾ × 8 inches

52

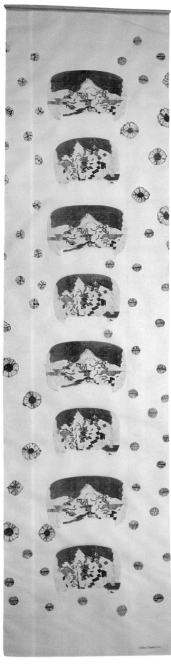

53

53
KATHERINE WESTPHAL
Disintegration of Mt. Fuji,
1977
Commercial silk organza,
Pellon; color-photocopy heat-
transfer
105 × 26¼ inches

54
KATHERINE WESTPHAL
Black Samurai, 1977
Commercial silk organza,
self-stick plastic tape, silk
cord; color-photocopy heat-
transfer, felt-tipped-pen
drawing
31 × 67 inches

55

54

56

56
KATHERINE WESTPHAL
Hawaiian Kitsch, 1978
Synthetic velvet, cotton;
quilted, color-photocopy
heat-transfer, felt-tipped-pen
drawing
90 × 56 inches

57
KATHERINE WESTPHAL
Giverny II, 1983
Paper, cotton, commercial
synthetic fabric with Lurex;
machine-stitched patchwork,
color-photocopy heat-
transfer, stamped
36½ × 48½ inches

58
KATHERINE WESTPHAL
Dragon Dancing Skirt, 1987
Paper, cotton; machine-
stitched patchwork, color-
photocopy heat-transfer,
stamped
82 × 40 inches

57

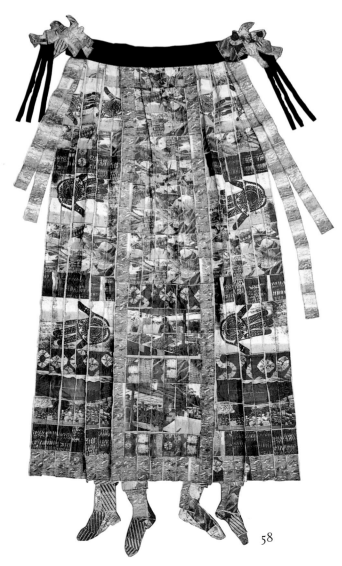

58

75

59

60, 61

59
KATHERINE WESTPHAL
Heavenly Fish, 1988
Synthetic raffia; crocheted
11¼ × 7 × 6¾ inches

60
KATHERINE WESTPHAL
Lotus Pond, 1988
Synthetic raffia, plastic
dinosaurs; crocheted
9 × 13¾ × 9½ inches

61
KATHERINE WESTPHAL
Water Garden, 1989–90
Synthetic raffia, plastic mos-
quitoes; crocheted
18½ × 10 × 11 inches

62
KATHERINE WESTPHAL
Shelley, 1989
Gourd, rice paper; color-
photocopy heat-transfer
9 × 9 × 9 inches

63
KATHERINE WESTPHAL
Juggling Benches, 1989
Synthetic raffia; crocheted
14½ × 7¾ inches (diam. at
bottom)

62

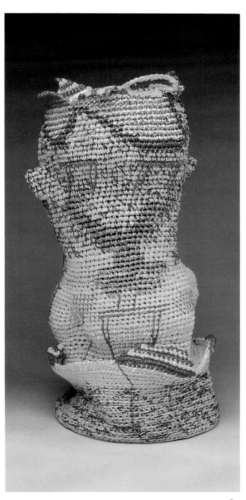

63

77

64

64
KATHERINE WESTPHAL
Vermillion Cliffs, 1989
Raffia, synthetic raffia;
crocheted
9½ × 7 inches (diam.)

65
KATHERINE WESTPHAL
Wesing in Guilin, Guilin,
1989
Raffia, synthetic raffia;
crocheted
18¾ × 8 × 8½ inches

66
KATHERINE WESTPHAL
Spotted Lilies, 1989
Bark, paper; machine-
stitched patchwork, color-
photocopy heat-transfer, felt-
tipped-pen, polyethylene
tubing necklace with paper
flowers and painted detail
38 × 28 inches

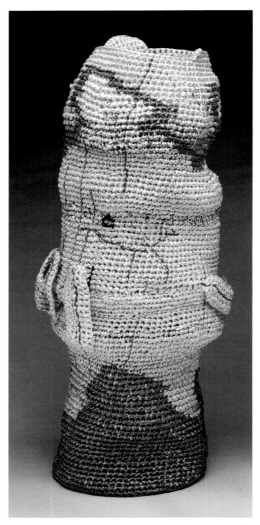

65

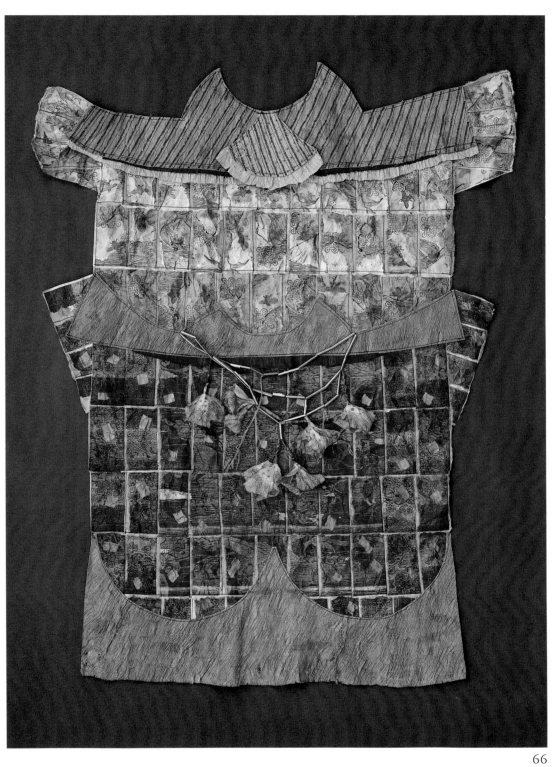

66

67

67
KATHERINE WESTPHAL
Ruffles, Beads, and Flowers,
1989
Bark, paper; machine-
stitched patchwork, color-
photocopy heat-transfer,
polyethylene tubing necklace
with polymer-clay beads,
paper flowers with painted
detail
31¾ × 23 inches

68
KATHERINE WESTPHAL
*Tiananmen Square, June
1989,* 1989
Gourd, paper, straw; color-
photocopy heat-transfer,
wrapped, tied
8¼ × 9½ × 9½ inches

68

69

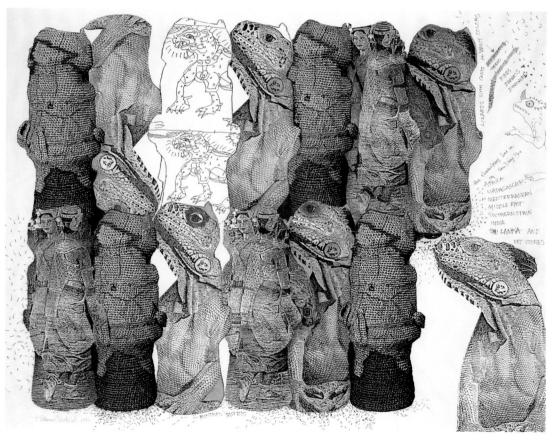

70

69
KATHERINE WESTPHAL
Belvedere, 1990
Gourd, paper; color-photo-
copy heat-transfer, painted
12 × 22 × 18 inches

70
KATHERINE WESTPHAL
Thirteen Baskets, 1990
Paper; photocopy, colored-
pencil and pen-and-ink
drawing
24³⁄₁₆ × 30³⁄₁₆ inches

71

72

74, 75, 73

71
KATHERINE WESTPHAL
Midnight, 1992
Raffia, synthetic raffia;
crocheted
10 × 10 × 8½ inches

72
KATHERINE WESTPHAL
Siren Song, 1993
Paper; machine-stitched
patchwork, photocopy heat-
transfer, dye-transfer crayon
38½ × 46¾ inches

73
KATHERINE WESTPHAL
Runner, 1993
Raffia, synthetic raffia;
crocheted
15¼ × 8¼ inches (diam.)

74
KATHERINE WESTPHAL
Greening, 1993
Raffia, synthetic raffia;
crocheted
12¾ × 7½ inches (diam.)

75
KATHERINE WESTPHAL
Sirens, 1993
Raffia, synthetic raffia;
crocheted
11⅞ × 9 inches (diam.)

76

77

78

79

76
KATHERINE WESTPHAL
Out of Focus in Attica, 1993
Paper; machine-stitched
patchwork, dip-dyed, photocopy heat-transfer, crayon
and felt-tipped-pen drawing
36¾ × 51¼ inches

77
KATHERINE WESTPHAL
*Fractured Greek Pots,
No. 8,* 1993
Paper; color-photocopy heat-
transfer, colored-pencil and
felt-tipped-pen drawing
22 × 30 inches

78
KATHERINE WESTPHAL
Lift Off, 1993
Raffia, synthetic raffia;
crocheted
11 × 7¾ inches (diam.)

79
KATHERINE WESTPHAL
Swimmers, 1993
Raffia, synthetic raffia;
crocheted
13½ × 9 inches (diam.)

84, 80

82, 81

83

80
KATHERINE WESTPHAL
Sun Dog, 1994
Raffia, synthetic raffia;
crocheted, polymer-clay
pendants
8 × 8½ inches (diam.)

81
KATHERINE WESTPHAL
Lillehammer, 1994
Raffia, synthetic raffia;
crocheted
11 × 8 inches (diam.)

82
KATHERINE WESTPHAL
Orbit, 1994
Raffia, synthetic raffia;
crocheted
10 × 7½ inches (diam.)

83
KATHERINE WESTPHAL
Wyoming, 1995
Raffia, synthetic raffia,
plastic fish; crocheted
11½ × 9½ inches (diam.)

84
KATHERINE WESTPHAL
Gifts from the Sea, 1996
Raffia, synthetic raffia;
crocheted, embroidered
10½ × 12 × 7½ inches

TIES THAT BIND

EDITOR: Judith A. Singsen

DESIGN: Gilbert Design Associates, Inc., Providence

PHOTOGRAPHY: Del Bogart (cat. nos. 1–6, 8–10, 13,
15–19, 21–30, 34–35, 38–39, 41–59, 63–67, 69–70,
72–76, 79–80, 84)
Dean Powell (cat. no. 20, courtesy Mobilia Gallery,
Cambridge, Massachusetts)
Dwight Primiano (cat. nos. 7, 11–12, 14, 31–33, 36–37,
40, 60–62, 68, 71, 77–78, 81–83)

PRINTING: Meridian Printing, East Greenwich

4,000 copies for the Museum of Art, Rhode Island
School of Design

October 1997